EASY START

In the pot

Written by Keith Gaines

Illustrated by Margaret de Souza

Nelson

"In the pot

I will put

a fat fish."

2

"In the pot.

In the pot."

"In the pot

I will put

a wet net."

4

"In the pot.

In the pot."

"In the pot

I will put

a smelly jelly."

"In the pot.

In the pot."

"In the pot
I will put
lots of pink paint."

"In the pot.

In the pot."

"Is it hot?"

"Yes, it is hot."

"Is it good?"

11